UNDAUNTED

Dear
Warrior –

As I pray over this journal, it is my hope that you will find it helpful as you grow closer to the Lord. May you remember to pick up your armor daily and walk your days UNdaunted!

Love In Christ,

Victoria Chapin

John 10:10

UNDAUNTED

A Prayer Journal

VICTORIA CHAPIN

Published by

UNdaunted: A Prayer Journal

First edition: April 2021

Book design by Frank Gutbrod

ISBN 978-1-954658-00-4

Published by The Well Publishers
www.seeyouatthewell.net/thewellpublishers

UNDAUNTED –

A Prayer Journal

ACKNOWLEDGMENTS

Just as I begin my days naming what I am thankful for, so will I start my first book with a heart filled with joy and gratitude. God has positioned me in the midst of people He knew I needed to complete this project, and I thank you all from the depths of my heart.

But first . . .

My Lord and Savior Jesus Christ. This Prayer Journal would not be possible had it not been inspired by the **Holy Spirit** and orchestrated by my loving Father.

And then . . .

The Well Publishers. Thank you **Kathy Bruins** for your wonderful coaching and editing skills. I can't thank you enough for all that you've selflessly done. Not only have you gone above and beyond in a professional sense, but you have been an amazing friend and inspiration to me. **Sandy Gould**, you have encouraged me from the moment I met you. Thank you for spurring me on to have my first book published by The Well Publishers. Your expertise and great connections are an integral part of completing this book. It has been a pleasure to work with you both.

Frank Gutbrod. Thank you for patiently working with me on the cover design and formatting to capture what I envisioned. It's been fun watching you bring it all together.

My Family. To my kids — Thank you for your encouraging words and being so flexible. All the 'fend for yourself' dinners and sacrifices you made were well worth it to help me fulfill this God given desire. To my husband Jim — I cannot put into words how grateful I am for all that you do day in and day out. Not only does it allow me to walk each day with purpose, but it motivates me to want to do more. Thank you for sacrificing and caring about my destiny and praying me through it. I'm so grateful that you walk by my side.

un·daunt·ed

/ˌənˈdôn(t)əd/

adjective

1. not intimidated or discouraged by difficulty, danger, or disappointment

You need to return to the truth of God's Word that will last forever, not meditate on circumstances that will fade and change. It is this truth that enables us to go into the future UNDAUNTED.

CHRISTINE CAINE

THE INSPIRATION

There was a time when rolling out of bed was just . . . hard. I knew in my mind that I should get up, but my physical body was not willing to break out of the hold that my blankets had on me. *Daunted* and depleted with no move in me, I prayed,

"God, just please get me through this day"

Sometimes it was "*the next hour*" or even "*the next 5 minutes*." And He would. Over and over, He did and I thanked Him every time. The more I showed gratitude, the easier it became. I found myself counting more than just that blessing, and soon after I was challenged to start my day thanking God for at least three things before I let my feet hit the floor.

Legs dangling, the side of my bed became a holy place. I didn't dare let my toes touch the floor until I uttered those words of thanksgiving. God met me there and our relationship deepened. Three things became more, and I started a journal with a list of 1000 gifts after reading Ann Voskamp's book *One Thousand Gifts: A Dare to Live Fully Right Where You Are.*

I went from feeling paralyzed in my bed to giving air high fives to God accompanied by shouts of

"Let's do this!"

Day after day, my list of blessings multiplied and so did my praise. I moved from speaking words of gratitude to singing songs of adoration. I longed to fill the morning with worship for my Lord, as it became oxygen to my spiritual breaths. I felt His presence and longed to hear Him more.

Enter his gates with thanksgiving and his courts with praise; give thanks to him and praise his name.

—Psalm 100:4 NIV

When I read this verse I thought, *That's it! This is why I'm a better listener when I start this way.* It wasn't an audible voice, but He would bring me to a place in the Word that was just what I needed in that moment, or in a book I was reading along with my Bible. Sometimes the lyrics of a song would speak to me so clearly, or He would place a thought in my head out of nowhere that was just too perfect to think that I came up with it. Does this ever happen to you?

I'll be real, friends; at times I heard things I didn't necessarily want to hear. God sometimes uncovered things that I didn't see in myself, but undeniably needed to. I had many humbling *"Okay, God"* moments; more than I'd like to admit as He called me to the repentance needed to know and hear Him more.

Immediately, something like scales fell from Saul's eyes, and he could see again

—ACTS 9:18A NIV

Have you experienced a time when you were reading Scripture (that you've likely read before) and suddenly the words are coming toward you in 3D? Did you scratch your head and think, *How have I missed that?* Or even better, you've had an epiphany. That was me as I dove into passages in God's Word after the weight of my sins had been lifted. My understanding increased as I humbled myself before Him and brought my shortcomings to the foot of the cross. I experienced God's forgiveness along with forgiveness in myself, which removed barriers and made me a sponge ready to absorb the Word like never before.

And here's how that led to the idea to publish this prayer journal.

I remember reading about the armor of God in Ephesians and thinking the symbolism was interesting, but it wasn't until I came to the Word positioned with thanksgiving, praise, and humility that I realized its power in spiritual warfare. Revelation came as I read the Word and pondered. I was not claiming and using these scriptures as fully as I could be. I had to dig deeper, jot things down, and reflect on what God had shown me that week.

Make your journaling into a book for others to use. I read this from my journal a few days before followed by a sketch with a layout of sections that had been inspired by the Holy Spirit. I noticed there were seven boxes in my diagram and was suddenly moved to count the pieces of armor on the page open in my Bible.

I'm a firm believer in numeric signs from God, and knowing that the number seven has significance in His Word, I counted again. At that moment I knew it was not coincidence: six pieces of physical armor with the seventh, prayer. Could it be that this prayer journal with seven sections was meant to be used to encourage others to a greater understanding of the power in the armor?

I've never completed a book before and thought, *How will I do this? Should this really be my first one? Where do I begin, Lord*? I wrote a prayer asking God to provide a way if this was something He wanted me to do. It took some time, but through a series of events and people He lined up for me to meet, as I write . . . it's finally happening! He is so patient and good, and I just know that **He wanted this for you**.

In a time when evil rises, God rises even higher and uses ordinary people to carry out His Word. All we have to do is be willing, and I was.

One day, as I journey with my very own copy, I'll be sure to write in the section Prayers Answered. I will praise and thank God for speaking this into existence and using my listening ear to hear what He wanted to be done with this project. I'm so excited for you to read of the relevancy in the armor of God and its power available to us for spiritual warfare.

We are to be warriors in the battle and He's provided these weapons to keep us UNDAUNTED!

THE ARMOR OF GOD

Finally, be strong in the Lord and in his mighty power. Put on the full armor of God, so that you can take your stand against the devil's schemes. For our struggle is not against flesh and blood, but against the rulers, against the authorities, against the powers of this dark world and against the spiritual forces of evil in the heavenly realms. Therefore put on the full armor of God, so that when the day of evil comes, you may be able to stand your ground, and after you have done everything, to stand. Stand firm then, with the belt of truth buckled around your waist, with the breastplate of righteousness in place, and with your feet fitted with the readiness that comes from the gospel of peace. In addition to all this, take up the shield of faith, with which you can extinguish all the flaming arrows of the evil one. Take the helmet of salvation and the sword of the Spirit, which is the word of God. And pray in the Spirit on all occasions with all kinds of prayers and requests. With this in mind, be alert and always keep on praying for all the Lord's people.

—EPHESIANS 6:10-18 NIV

Belt of Truth

The Belt of Truth is the first piece of armor listed, and I believe that is on purpose. Truth comes first because without it, all the other pieces of armor would be lacking. There can be no righteousness, peace and so on without truth. Just as the belt of a Roman soldier held the sword and the other pieces of armor to the body, so truth holds a life with Christ secure. The Bible is the book of truth so it's important to be in God's Word daily.

Breastplate of Righteousness

Righteousness comes through faith in Jesus Christ to all who believe. Since our flesh fails and we have no righteousness aside from Jesus, it is He who protects us from the world. As a breastplate protected the Roman soldiers from their foes, similarly the breastplate of Christ protects us from evil. Strap on the righteousness of Christ daily for He is our Savior and Protector.

Sandals with the Gospel of Peace

It was important for Roman soldiers' feet to be prepared to march in long battles, so they were fitted with thick-soled sandals with straps that supported their ankles and spiked bottoms to secure their steps. To walk in readiness with the Lord, we must strap on the gospel of peace, that is the Good News, so that we are fully prepared. When we embrace what Christ did on the cross for us, it gives us security and a firm foundation to base our lives on.

Shield of Faith

A Roman soldier's shield was the first layer of protection. Fiery arrows could not penetrate this important weapon of defense. As believers, our faith is the shield that protects when we are attacked on all sides. To remain faithful, we must shield ourselves with God's power as it's our protection against the enemy's schemes.

Helmet of Salvation

Without salvation in Jesus Christ, there is no victory. Without protection of the face and head, the Roman soldier's armor would be incomplete. I can't imagine going into battle with full body armor, but nothing covering the head. The Helmet of Salvation protects us not only from the battle against sin and the tempter, but the battle with our own mind. Let's put our helmets of salvation on and be grateful for what Christ did on the cross to allow us our freedom.

Sword of the Spirit

The Sword of the Spirit is the Word of God, and there is no better way to go after the lies and schemes of the enemy than with the Holy Scriptures. The Word of God is sharp and can pierce through the darkness of this world like no other weapon. Jesus modeled this when Satan tried to tempt Him in the desert. We must consume God's Word so that we become adept in using it.

Prayer

When we put on the Armor of God we are clothing ourselves for battle, but we are not to go into it alone. Prayer is the seventh component and connects us to our Commander in Chief. We get direction from Him along the way and He renews our strength. Prayer is one of our best weapons as it's used on offense and defense. The Word says to pray in the Spirit **at all times**. Praying in the Spirit is powerful and a necessary companion to the Armor of God.

HOW TO USE YOUR JOURNAL

The UNDAUNTED prayer journal is for you, which means you can go at your own pace. There are enough journal pages for it to be used consistently for 90 days if you cover all seven sections per day. You might like to spend a longer period of time in the morning in prayer or use it at night before bed. Perhaps keeping it open throughout the day doing a section or two at a time will work best for you. If you spend more time in prayer on the weekends, using it as a weekend journal is an option too. Although you can customize it to your schedule, I encourage you to stick with it and be consistent with the time you choose. It's certainly not meant as another thing to simply check off your "to do list" for the day, but keeping your Spirit-led appointments with God will help you get to know and hear Him more. It's all about your relationship with Jesus.

SECTION 1 – *Thanksgiving*

In everything give thanks;
for this is the will of God for you in Christ Jesus.

—1 THESSALONIANS 5:18 NASB

For most of us there are so many things to be grateful for that all of our blessings would not fit in the daily box marked thanksgiving; so to start, I suggest listing at least three per day. If you're like me, there will be a constant flow until one day it slows. Does this mean there isn't much else to note? Not at all, but it might be time for us to slow down, shift our perspectives to see a bigger picture.

When we purposefully look to see the beauty in nature, for example, we notice an array of colors and feel warmth in the fall leaves as we drive down the highway to our destination. What a magnificent piece of art we get to admire as we go on a long trip. Too often, I did not notice things like this until I started to list them. One time I remember viewing an annoying drip in the kitchen sink as a blessing because I thought about people without clean running water. *They would rejoice in that sound*, I thought. I pray that when you work on this section, it will become a treasure hunt where you'll find many jewels.

SECTION 2 – *Praise and Worship*

Blessed be your glorious name,
and may it be exalted above all blessings and praise.

—NEHEMIAH 9:5 NIV

Praise and worship has to be one of my favorite things to do when spending time with God. Even now as I type there's a melody ringing in my head. I can't keep from praising the Lord because His love is so amazing. There are days that I just want to shout and sing and dance. While doing so brings much joy, it also brings protection. Praise and worship are weapons used to thwart the enemy, and I'm not afraid to use them!

Most days I begin my time with the Lord listening to worship music. As I close my eyes and let the music take over, the Spirit often moves me towards His presence. If you don't do this already, I highly recommend it. During your time of worship, write down lyrics that resonate with you or thoughts that are brought forth as you praise Him. I've also experienced times when I've simply desired to sit in silence speaking words of praise to Christ our King, and then I write those down as if writing Him a note of adoration. Whatever you do to give glory to our God can be noted here in this box.

SECTION 3 – *Humble Confession*

For all have sinned,
and come short of the glory of God.

—ROMANS 3:23 KJV

Give me an **S!** Give me an **I!** Give me an **N!** What does that spell? Okay, so who really wants to cheer about sin? Do we even want to acknowledge it at times? It's definitely not something to celebrate, right? But FREEDOM from sin surely is, and it's my prayer that this section will become for you what it has for me; a place where chains are broken. What was one of my least favorite boxes to fill in has become one of the most necessary to hear God more clearly.

As you approach this box, it's important to go there. Let humility wash over you so you're prepared to confess the obvious shortcomings in your day. You're not alone in this as we all have them. It might be a reaction you had towards something that happened and could have been handled better, an argument you took part in, or something bigger. Perhaps it's something only you and God know about, like a thought you had that's not exactly holy. Write it down and give it to God because He knows anyway. It's those prideful or judgemental thoughts that I didn't pay attention to until I said, "God, please show me anything in my life that could hinder me from hearing You more clearly." While it's not been fun to face at times, I'm so thankful He does remove the blinders, and even more thankful for the blood that was shed on the cross so I could be forgiven.

SECTION 4 – *God's Word*

For the word of God is living and powerful,
and sharper than any two-edged sword,
piercing even to the division of soul and spirit,
and of joints and marrow,
and is a discerner of the thoughts
and intents of the heart.

—HEBREWS 4:12 NKJV

There are times when it's a challenge to fully express the greatness in something, and one of those times is now. I'm at a loss for words to describe the significance in God's Word. God himself is sovereign so the verity that Scripture is God-breathed is just awe-inspiring. I can't imagine not having the Bible to guide me through life. I felt lost before it became a crucial part of my days. It's truly my sustenance, and I experience an unbalance in my day if I don't consume it.

You'll notice that this box is a bigger space than other sections, and that was done for you on purpose. Some days one verse will stand out and you may want to write it all down and memorize it. Another time it might be a whole paragraph that touches your heart or challenges you, so you'll need more space. If you keep the journal open and use it throughout the day, it's a great place to jot down the book and scripture references so you have it handy to look up when you have more time. I've found it works well as a place to collect favorite scriptures and to refer back to them as you study and reflect on God's Word.

SECTION 5 – *Reflection*

And don't for a minute let this book of
The Revelation be out of mind.
Ponder and meditate on it day and night.

—JOSHUA 1:8 MSG

Across from the God's Word section is Reflection, and it's the same size and strategically placed. The neat thing about them being side by side is there's more than one way to journal in this area. You can either work from top to bottom on the left side writing your Scripture down and then writing what God revealed to you across from it on the right side; or you can use it as one square writing Scripture with revelation flowing across both pages.

Let the Holy Spirit lead and you'll be amazed some days at what God shows you through His Word. As you seek to hear Him more, He will open your eyes to things you've not seen or give you a deeper understanding of who He is and how He loves. I have story after story of discoveries that came during this time of reflection. If a thought or vision pops into your mind, write it down, even if you don't think it has anything to do with what you read. It could be something God's wanting you to ponder or pray about. I'm so excited for you to experience jaw-dropping moments with Him!

SECTION 6 – *The Asking*

With all prayer and petition pray [with specific requests] at all times [on every occasion and in every season] in the Spirit, and with this in view, stay alert with all perseverance and petition [interceding in prayer] for all God's people.

—EPHESIANS 6:18 AMP

Have you told someone that you would pray for them and then never did? I have. It was not intentional, but I either forgot or just got busy. It is comforting to hear the words "I'll pray for you," but even more so when we experience the kind of comfort that God gives because that prayer was heard and answered. So many people need prayer and it can be overwhelming to try and cover everyone's requests. I want to encourage you that if you're open and willing, God will often give you a burden for whom He wants you to intercede. You might read about a concern in a social media group or page, or someone might ask you personally to pray. The purpose of The Asking section is to write those names down and lift their concerns to the Lord with the authority given to us through Christ Jesus.

I've heard it said when we take our eyes off from ourselves and put them on others, our problems aren't as big and our needs are often met. I've seen this happen with prayer over and over. To clarify, there is nothing wrong with asking God for provision and answers for you and your family. In fact, God tells us to in the Scripture above. He even says that we don't have, because we don't ask. So ask away and pray that God's will be done on earth as it is in heaven. And when you don't know exactly what words to pray, God's Word says that the Holy Spirit will intercede through wordless groans.This is praying in the Spirit and it is for all people. Isn't that amazing?

SECTION 7 – *Prayers Answered*

And my God will supply all your needs
according to His riches in glory in Christ Jesus.

—PHILIPPIANS 4:19 NASB

I know it might date me, but one of my favorite songs back in the 90's was by Wayne Watson called *When God's People Pray*. I was comforted when I heard the artist sing of bringing our earthly pain to the doors of Heaven through prayer. It was a time when I needed the Father's ear like never before, and I knew He would not turn from me. Some of my prayers were answered as I believed they would, while others were answered quite differently than I hoped. But I realized that God's "no" is still an answer ... the best answer. I may not have seen it then, but down the road, it became much clearer.

What thrills me is the part of the song that names miracles and how we can't explain them away. I know this to be true with signs and wonders too, because my life has been full of them. I've experienced God at work in undeniable ways, too many to be mere coincidence. Over time, we can tend to forget how events played out in our lives, but we don't want to miss giving God the glory for what He's done, right? The last section in this journal is a place for you to remember how God answered your prayers. It could be your "yes" that was the miracle, your "no" that was a sign, or an answer that leaves you wondering; whatever it is, write it down so you can look back on God's goodness, grace, and provision.

Listening vs Talking

Listen and hear my voice;
pay attention and hear what I say.

—ISAIAH 28:23 NIV

If you were to ask God what the communication is like in your relationship with Him, would He say that you do more talking or listening? I am a talker, but the more time I spend in His presence listening, the more in tune I am to His voice.

At the top of each section you will see two symbols. The ear represents listening and the chat bubble, talking. When you journal and spend time with the Lord, pay attention to what you did more of in each section, and circle that symbol. It could change as the Spirit leads, and there might be some days you circle both. It is my prayer that your time with God becomes a conversation.

Armor Symbols

At the bottom of the journal pages, you will see the first six pieces of the Armor of God. As you journey through your prayers using the sections in which to write, reflect on which piece(s) of armor best kept you UNDAUNTED that day or week. Go ahead and circle the symbol or jot a note next to it. I found myself sometimes drawing a line from the symbol to the section that it was most related to that day. For example: you could draw a line from the helmet of salvation to the Thanksgiving section if you were thanking God for your friend accepting Jesus!

YOUR JOURNEY

Thanksgiving

Praise & Worship

Humility & Confession

God’s Word

Put on the full armor of God so you can stand your ground!

Reflection

The Asking

Prayers Answered

What pieces of armor were used to keep you UNDAUNTED?

DAY 02

Thanksgiving

Praise & Worship

Humility & Confession

God's Word

Put on the full armor of God so you can stand your ground!

Reflection

The Asking

Prayers Answered

What pieces of armor were used to keep you UNDAUNTED?

DAY 03

Thanksgiving

Praise & Worship

Humility & Confession

God's Word

Put on the full armor of God so you can stand your ground!

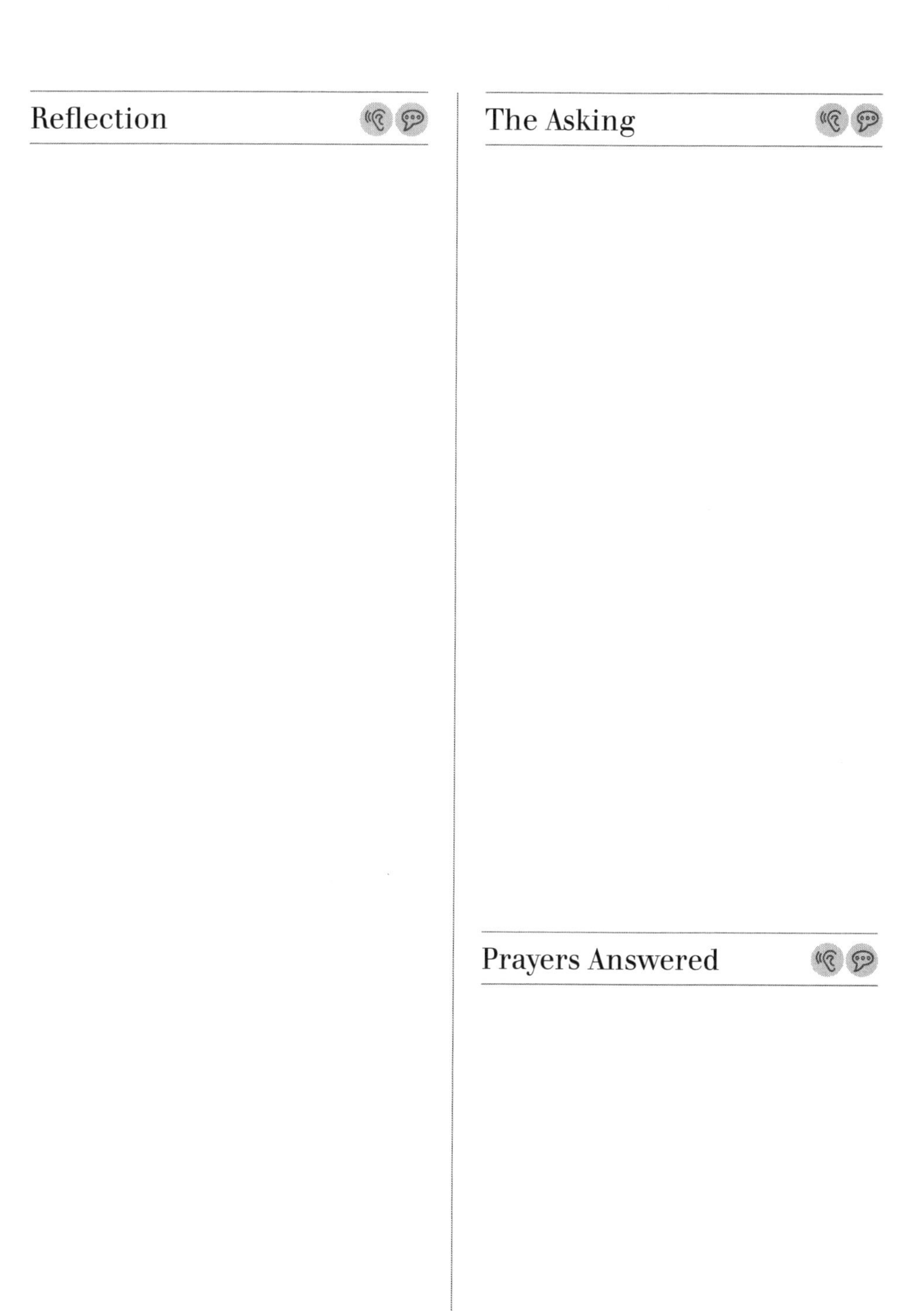

Reflection

The Asking

Prayers Answered

What pieces of armor were used to keep you UNDAUNTED?

DAY 04

Thanksgiving

God's Word

Praise & Worship

Humility & Confession

Put on the full armor of God so you can stand your ground!

Reflection

The Asking

Prayers Answered

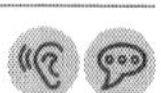

What pieces of armor were used to keep you UNDAUNTED?

DAY 05 Thanksgiving

Praise & Worship

Humility & Confession

God's Word

Put on the full armor of God so you can stand your ground!

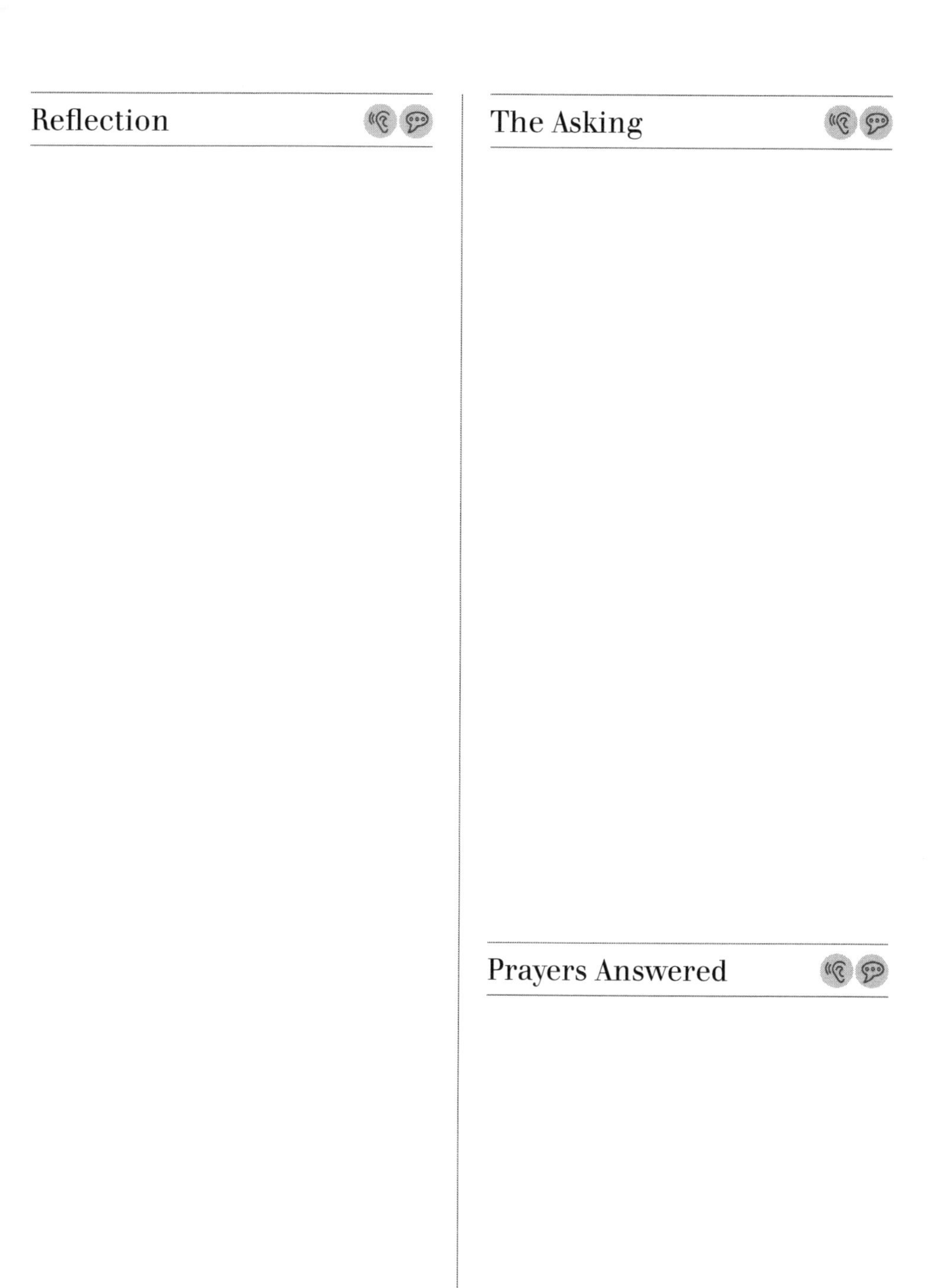

Reflection

The Asking

Prayers Answered

What pieces of armor were used to keep you UNDAUNTED?

DAY 06

Thanksgiving

God's Word

Praise & Worship

Humility & Confession

Put on the full armor of God so you can stand your ground!

Reflection

The Asking

Prayers Answered

What pieces of armor were used to keep you UNDAUNTED?

DAY 07

Thanksgiving

Praise & Worship

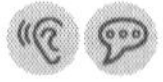

Humility & Confession

God's Word

Put on the full armor of God so you can stand your ground!

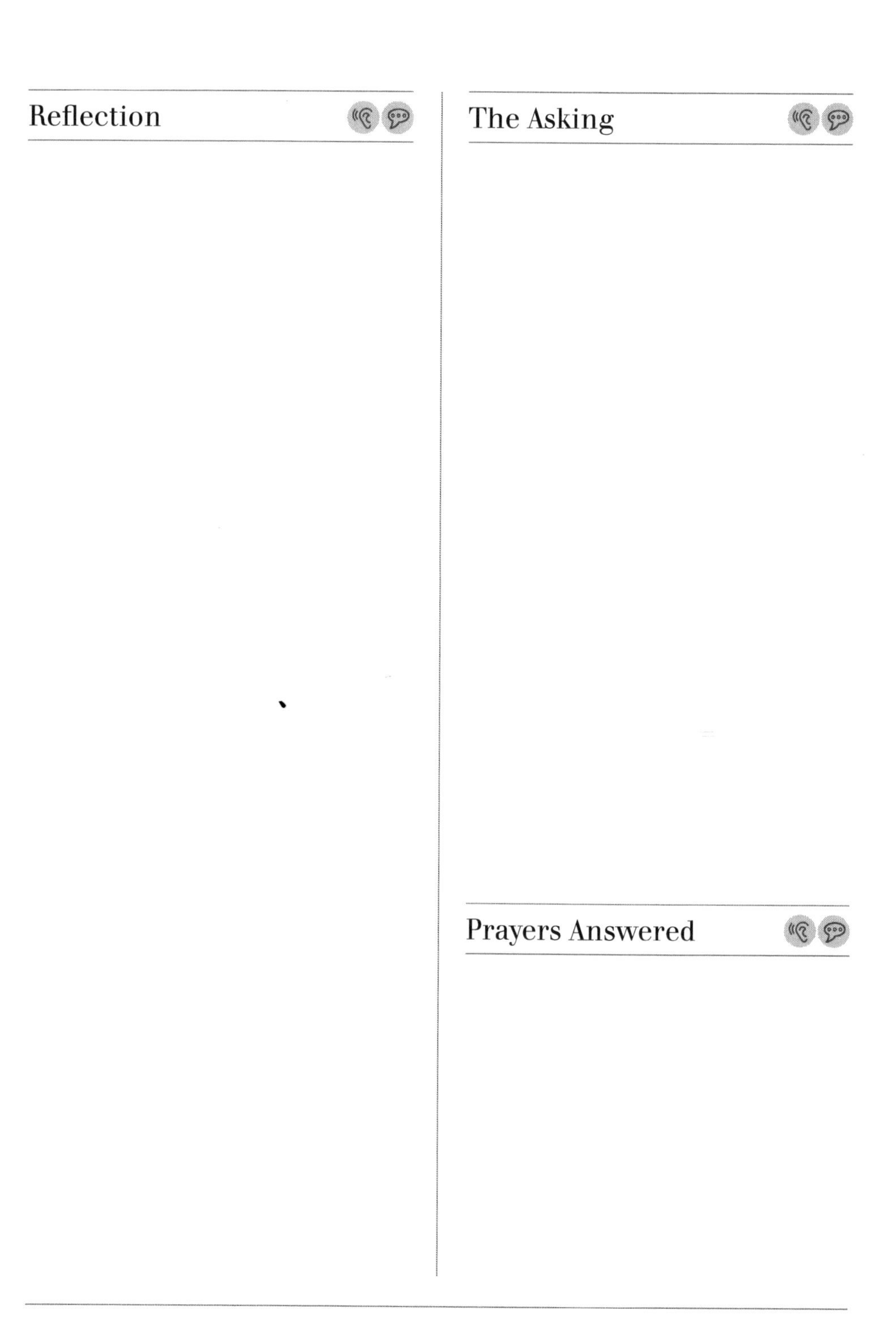

Reflection

The Asking

Prayers Answered

What pieces of armor were used to keep you UNDAUNTED?

DAY 08

Thanksgiving

Praise & Worship

Humility & Confession

God's Word

Put on the full armor of God so you can stand your ground!

Reflection

The Asking

Prayers Answered

What pieces of armor were used to keep you UNDAUNTED?

DAY 09

Thanksgiving

God's Word

Praise & Worship

Humility & Confession

Put on the full armor of God so you can stand your ground!

Reflection

The Asking

Prayers Answered

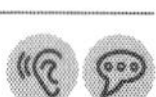

What pieces of armor were used to keep you UNDAUNTED?

DAY 10

Thanksgiving

God's Word

Praise & Worship 

Humility & Confession 

Put on the full armor of God so you can stand your ground!

Reflection

The Asking

Prayers Answered

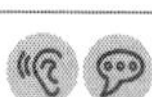

What pieces of armor were used to keep you UNDAUNTED?

DAY 11

Thanksgiving

God's Word

Praise & Worship

Humility & Confession

Put on the full armor of God so you can stand your ground!

Reflection

The Asking

Prayers Answered

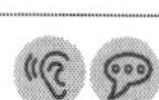

What pieces of armor were used to keep you UNDAUNTED?

DAY 12

Thanksgiving

God's Word

Praise & Worship

Humility & Confession

Put on the full armor of God so you can stand your ground!

Reflection

The Asking

Prayers Answered

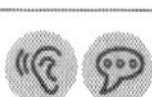

What pieces of armor were used to keep you UNDAUNTED?

DAY 13

Thanksgiving

God's Word

Praise & Worship

Humility & Confession

Put on the full armor of God so you can stand your ground!

Reflection

The Asking

Prayers Answered

What pieces of armor were used to keep you UNDAUNTED?

DAY 14

Thanksgiving

Praise & Worship

Humility & Confession

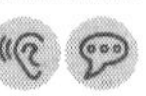

God's Word

Put on the full armor of God so you can stand your ground!

Reflection

The Asking

Prayers Answered

DAY 15

Thanksgiving

Praise & Worship

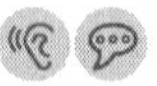

Humility & Confession

God's Word

Put on the full armor of God so you can stand your ground!

Reflection 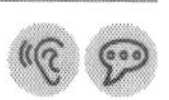

The Asking 

Prayers Answered 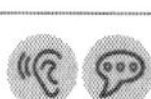

What pieces of armor were used to keep you UNDAUNTED?

DAY 16 Thanksgiving

God's Word

Praise & Worship

Humility & Confession

Put on the full armor of God so you can stand your ground!

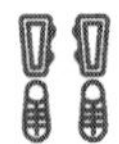

Reflection 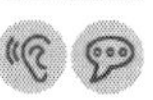

The Asking 

Prayers Answered 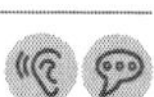

What pieces of armor were used to keep you UNDAUNTED?

DAY 17

Thanksgiving

God's Word

Praise & Worship

Humility & Confession

Put on the full armor of God so you can stand your ground!

Reflection

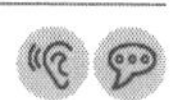

The Asking

Prayers Answered

What pieces of armor were used to keep you UNDAUNTED?

DAY 18

Thanksgiving

God's Word

Praise & Worship

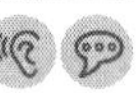

Humility & Confession

Put on the full armor of God so you can stand your ground!

Reflection

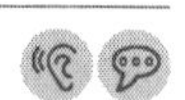

The Asking

Prayers Answered

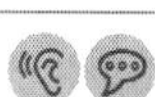

What pieces of armor were used to keep you UNDAUNTED?

DAY 19

Thanksgiving

God's Word

Praise & Worship

Humility & Confession

Put on the full armor of God so you can stand your ground!

Reflection

The Asking

Prayers Answered

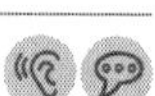

What pieces of armor were used to keep you UNDAUNTED?

Thanksgiving

Praise & Worship

Humility & Confession

God's Word

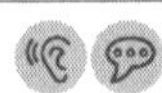

Put on the full armor of God so you can stand your ground!

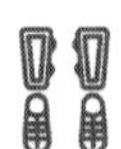

Reflection

The Asking

Prayers Answered

What pieces of armor were used to keep you UNDAUNTED?

DAY 21

Thanksgiving

Praise & Worship

Humility & Confession

God's Word

Put on the full armor of God so you can stand your ground!

Reflection

The Asking

Prayers Answered

DAY 22

Thanksgiving

Praise & Worship

Humility & Confession

God's Word

Put on the full armor of God so you can stand your ground!

Reflection

The Asking

Prayers Answered

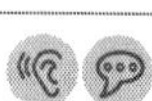

What pieces of armor were used to keep you UNDAUNTED?

DAY 23

Thanksgiving

Praise & Worship

Humility & Confession

God's Word

Put on the full armor of God so you can stand your ground!

Reflection

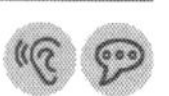

The Asking

Prayers Answered

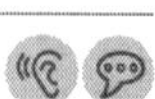

What pieces of armor were used to keep you UNDAUNTED?

Thanksgiving

Praise & Worship

Humility & Confession

God's Word

Put on the full armor of God so you can stand your ground!

Reflection

The Asking

Prayers Answered

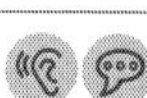

What pieces of armor were used to keep you UNDAUNTED?

DAY 25

Thanksgiving

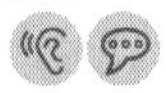

Praise & Worship

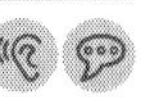

Humility & Confession

God's Word

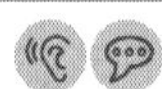

Put on the full armor of God so you can stand your ground!

Reflection

The Asking

Prayers Answered

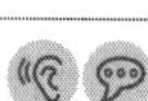

What pieces of armor were used to keep you UNDAUNTED?

DAY 26

Thanksgiving

God's Word

Praise & Worship

Humility & Confession

Put on the full armor of God so you can stand your ground!

Reflection

The Asking

Prayers Answered

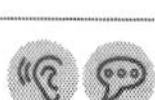

What pieces of armor were used to keep you UNDAUNTED?

DAY 27

Thanksgiving

God's Word

Praise & Worship

Humility & Confession

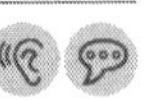

Put on the full armor of God so you can stand your ground!

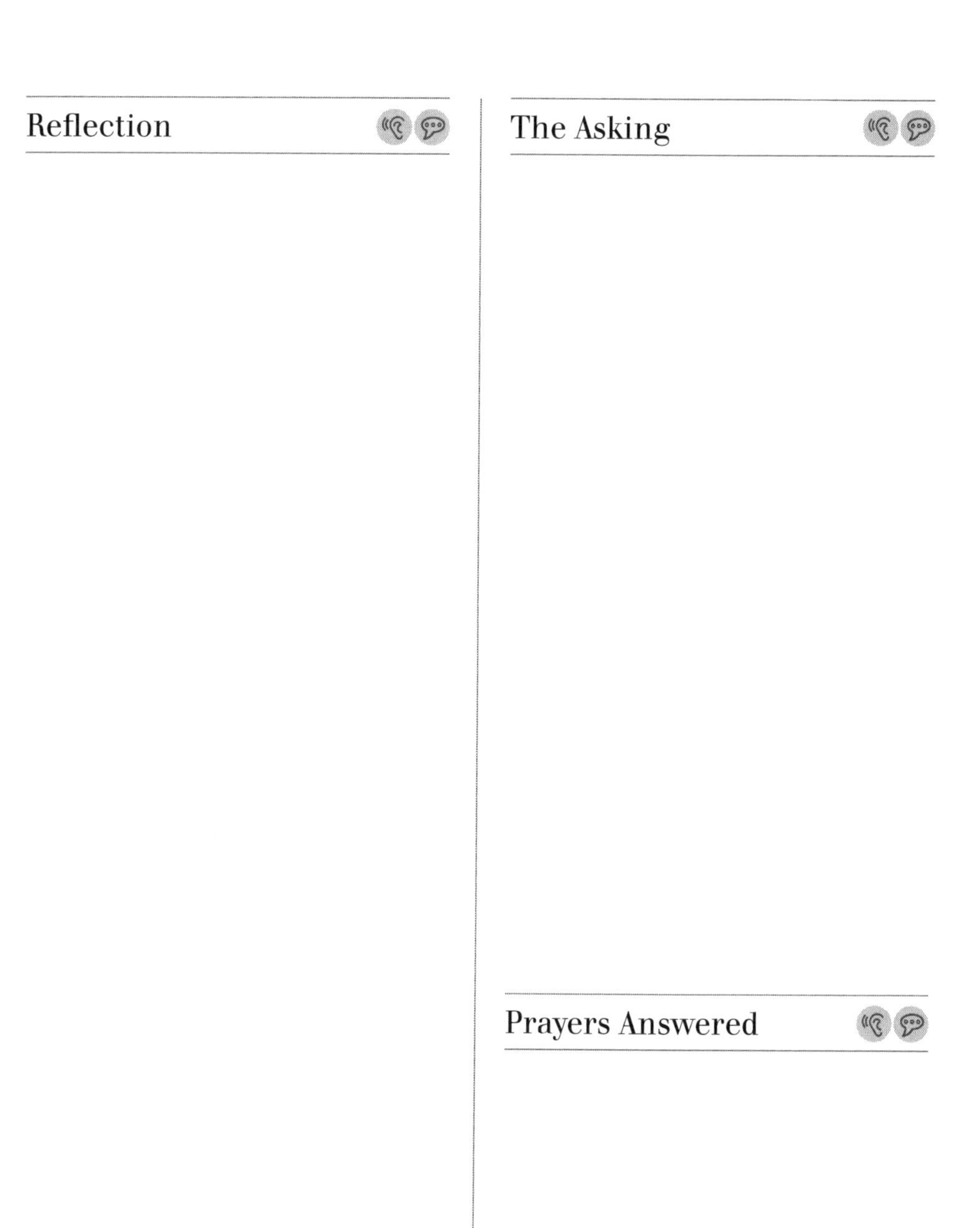

Reflection

The Asking

Prayers Answered

What pieces of armor were used to keep you UNDAUNTED?

DAY 28

Thanksgiving

Praise & Worship

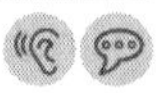

Humility & Confession

God's Word

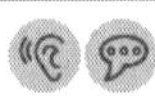

Put on the full armor of God so you can stand your ground!

Reflection

The Asking

Prayers Answered

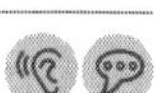

DAY 29

Thanksgiving

God's Word

Praise & Worship

Humility & Confession

Put on the full armor of God so you can stand your ground!

Reflection

The Asking

Prayers Answered

What pieces of armor were used to keep you UNDAUNTED?

DAY 30

Thanksgiving

Praise & Worship

Humility & Confession

God's Word

Put on the full armor of God so you can stand your ground!

Reflection

The Asking

Prayers Answered

What pieces of armor were used to keep you UNDAUNTED?

DAY 31

Thanksgiving

God's Word

Praise & Worship

Humility & Confession

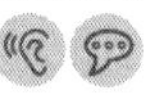

Put on the full armor of God so you can stand your ground!

Reflection

The Asking

Prayers Answered

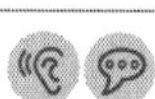

What pieces of armor were used to keep you UNDAUNTED?

DAY 32

Thanksgiving

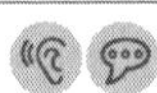

God's Word

Praise & Worship

Humility & Confession

Put on the full armor of God so you can stand your ground!

Reflection

The Asking

Prayers Answered

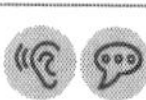

What pieces of armor were used to keep you UNDAUNTED?

DAY 33

Thanksgiving

Praise & Worship

Humility & Confession

God's Word

Put on the full armor of God so you can stand your ground!

Reflection

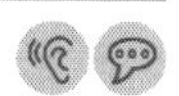

The Asking

Prayers Answered

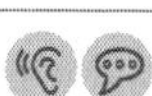

What pieces of armor were used to keep you UNDAUNTED?

Thanksgiving

Praise & Worship 

Humility & Confession 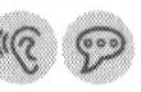

God's Word 

Put on the full armor of God so you can stand your ground!

Reflection

The Asking

Prayers Answered

What pieces of armor were used to keep you UNDAUNTED?

DAY 35

Thanksgiving

Praise & Worship

Humility & Confession

God's Word

Put on the full armor of God so you can stand your ground!

Reflection

The Asking

Prayers Answered

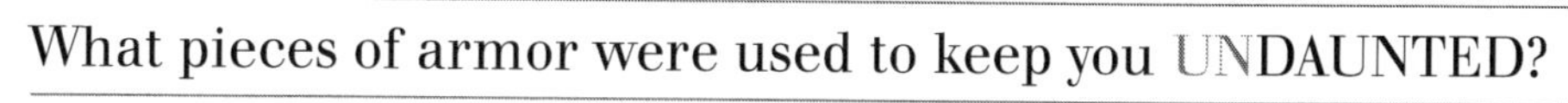

What pieces of armor were used to keep you UNDAUNTED?

DAY 36

Thanksgiving

God's Word

Praise & Worship

Humility & Confession

Put on the full armor of God so you can stand your ground!

Reflection

The Asking

Prayers Answered

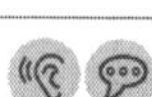

What pieces of armor were used to keep you UNDAUNTED?

DAY 37

Thanksgiving

God's Word

Praise & Worship

Humility & Confession

Put on the full armor of God so you can stand your ground!

Reflection 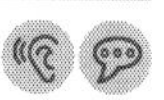

The Asking 

Prayers Answered 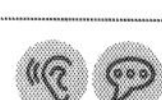

What pieces of armor were used to keep you UNDAUNTED?

DAY 38

Thanksgiving

Praise & Worship 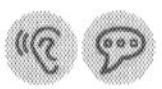

Humility & Confession 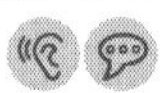

God's Word

Put on the full armor of God so you can stand your ground!

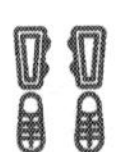

Reflection

The Asking

Prayers Answered

What pieces of armor were used to keep you UNDAUNTED?

DAY 39

Thanksgiving

Praise & Worship

Humility & Confession

God's Word

Put on the full armor of God so you can stand your ground!

Reflection

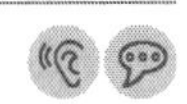

The Asking

Prayers Answered

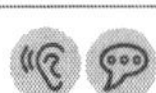

What pieces of armor were used to keep you UNDAUNTED?

DAY 40

Thanksgiving

Praise & Worship

Humility & Confession

God's Word

Put on the full armor of God so you can stand your ground!

Reflection

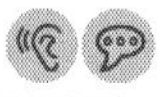

The Asking

Prayers Answered

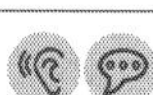

What pieces of armor were used to keep you UNDAUNTED?

Thanksgiving

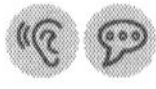

Praise & Worship

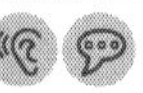

Humility & Confession

God's Word

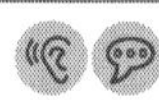

Put on the full armor of God so you can stand your ground!

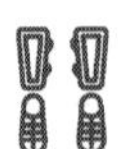

Reflection

The Asking

Prayers Answered

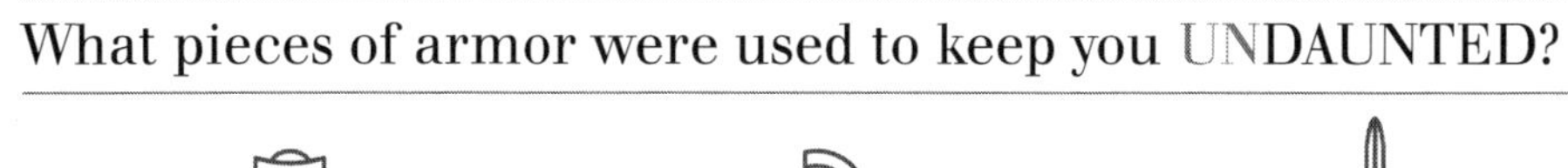

What pieces of armor were used to keep you UNDAUNTED?

Thanksgiving

Praise & Worship 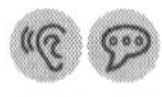

Humility & Confession 

God's Word 

Put on the full armor of God so you can stand your ground!

Reflection

The Asking

Prayers Answered

What pieces of armor were used to keep you UNDAUNTED?

DAY 43

Thanksgiving

Praise & Worship 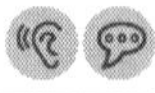

Humility & Confession 

God's Word 

Put on the full armor of God so you can stand your ground!

Reflection

The Asking

Prayers Answered

What pieces of armor were used to keep you UNDAUNTED?

Thanksgiving

God's Word

Praise & Worship

Humility & Confession

Put on the full armor of God so you can stand your ground!

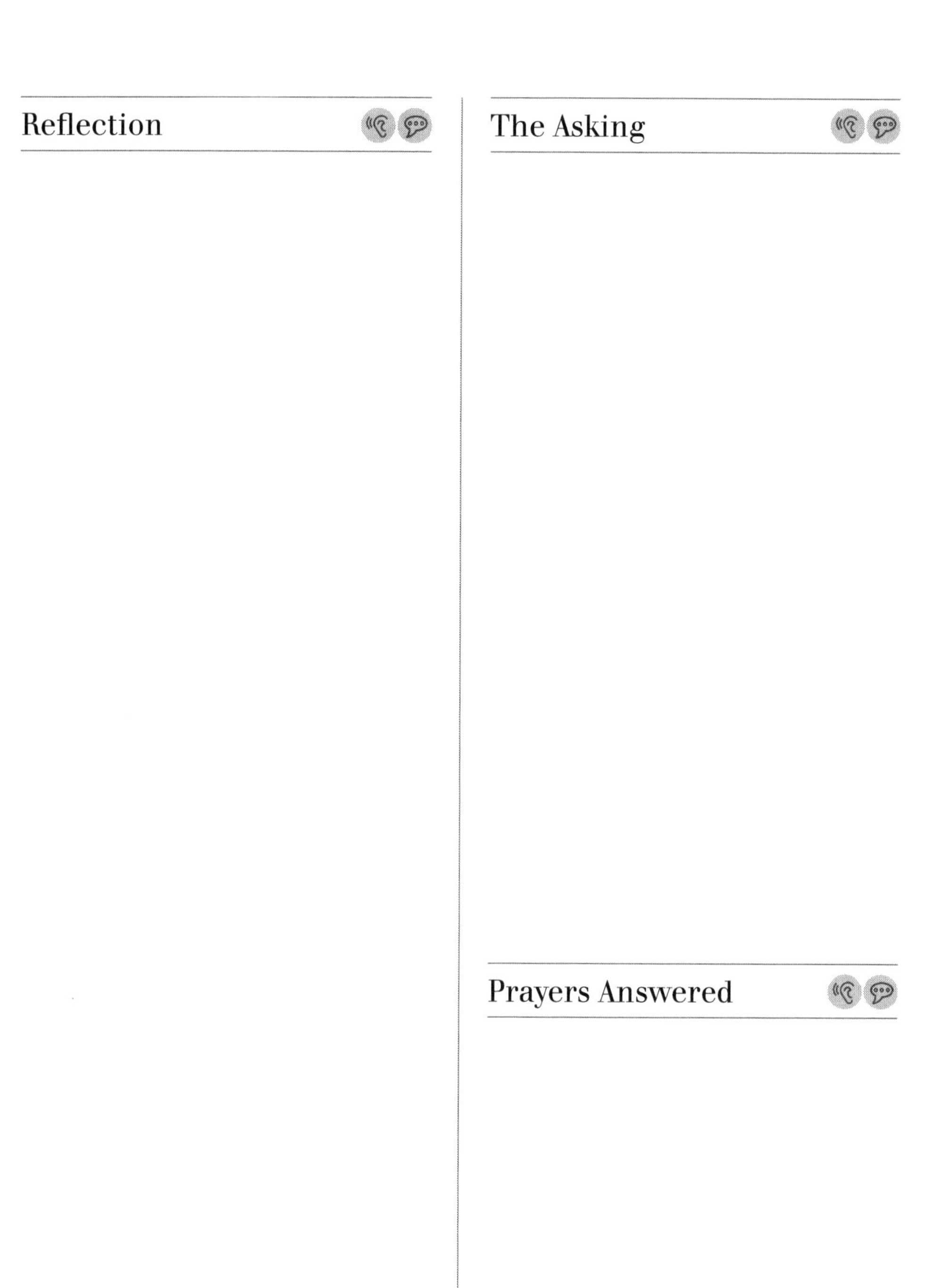

Reflection

The Asking

Prayers Answered

What pieces of armor were used to keep you UNDAUNTED?

DAY 45

Thanksgiving

God's Word

Praise & Worship

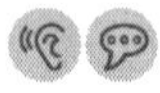

Humility & Confession

Put on the full armor of God so you can stand your ground!

Reflection

The Asking

Prayers Answered

What pieces of armor were used to keep you UNDAUNTED?

Thanksgiving

God's Word

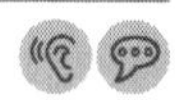

Praise & Worship

Humility & Confession

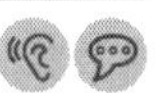

Put on the full armor of God so you can stand your ground!

Reflection

The Asking

Prayers Answered

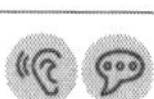

What pieces of armor were used to keep you UNDAUNTED?

Thanksgiving 

Praise & Worship 

Humility & Confession 

God’s Word 

Put on the full armor of God so you can stand your ground!

Reflection

The Asking

Prayers Answered

What pieces of armor were used to keep you UNDAUNTED?

Thanksgiving

God's Word

Praise & Worship

Humility & Confession

Put on the full armor of God so you can stand your ground!

Reflection

The Asking

Prayers Answered

What pieces of armor were used to keep you UNDAUNTED?

Thanksgiving

Praise & Worship 

Humility & Confession 

God's Word 

Put on the full armor of God so you can stand your ground!

Reflection

The Asking

Prayers Answered

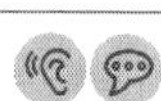

What pieces of armor were used to keep you UNDAUNTED?

DAY 50

Thanksgiving

Praise & Worship

Humility & Confession

God's Word

Put on the full armor of God so you can stand your ground!

Reflection

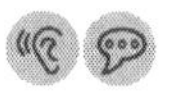

The Asking

Prayers Answered

What pieces of armor were used to keep you UNDAUNTED?

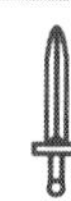

DAY 51

Thanksgiving

Praise & Worship

Humility & Confession

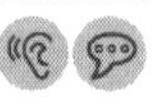

God's Word

Put on the full armor of God so you can stand your ground!

Reflection

The Asking

Prayers Answered

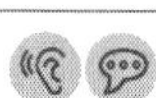

What pieces of armor were used to keep you UNDAUNTED?

DAY 52

Thanksgiving

God's Word

Praise & Worship

Humility & Confession

Put on the full armor of God so you can stand your ground!

Reflection

The Asking

Prayers Answered

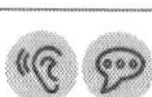

What pieces of armor were used to keep you UNDAUNTED?

DAY 53

Thanksgiving

God's Word

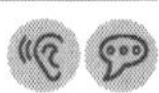

Praise & Worship

Humility & Confession

Put on the full armor of God so you can stand your ground!

Reflection

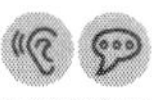

The Asking

Prayers Answered

What pieces of armor were used to keep you UNDAUNTED?

DAY 54

Thanksgiving

Praise & Worship

Humility & Confession

God's Word

Put on the full armor of God so you can stand your ground!

Reflection

The Asking

Prayers Answered

What pieces of armor were used to keep you UNDAUNTED?

DAY 55

Thanksgiving

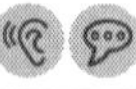

God's Word

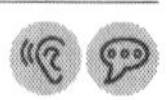

Praise & Worship

Humility & Confession

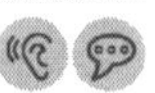

Put on the full armor of God so you can stand your ground!

Reflection

The Asking

Prayers Answered

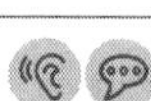

What pieces of armor were used to keep you UNDAUNTED?

DAY 56

Thanksgiving

God's Word

Praise & Worship

Humility & Confession

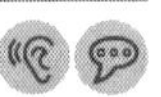

Put on the full armor of God so you can stand your ground!

Reflection

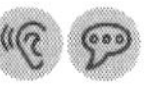

The Asking

Prayers Answered

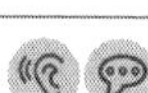

What pieces of armor were used to keep you UNDAUNTED?

DAY 57

Thanksgiving 

God's Word 

Praise & Worship 

Humility & Confession 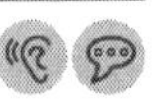

Put on the full armor of God so you can stand your ground!

Reflection

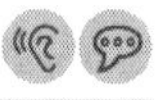

The Asking

Prayers Answered

What pieces of armor were used to keep you UNDAUNTED?

DAY 58

Thanksgiving

Praise & Worship

Humility & Confession

God's Word

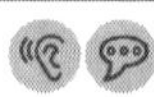

Put on the full armor of God so you can stand your ground!

Reflection

The Asking

Prayers Answered

What pieces of armor were used to keep you UNDAUNTED?

DAY 59

Thanksgiving

God's Word

Praise & Worship

Humility & Confession

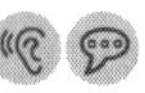

Put on the full armor of God so you can stand your ground!

Reflection

The Asking

Prayers Answered

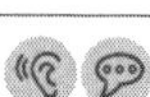

What pieces of armor were used to keep you UNDAUNTED?

DAY 60

Thanksgiving

God's Word

Praise & Worship

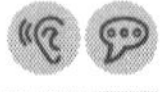

Humility & Confession

Put on the full armor of God so you can stand your ground!

Reflection

The Asking

Prayers Answered

What pieces of armor were used to keep you UNDAUNTED?

Thanksgiving

Praise & Worship

Humility & Confession

God's Word

Put on the full armor of God so you can stand your ground!

Reflection

The Asking

Prayers Answered

What pieces of armor were used to keep you UNDAUNTED?

DAY 62

Thanksgiving

Praise & Worship

Humility & Confession

God's Word

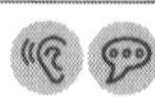

Put on the full armor of God so you can stand your ground!

Reflection

The Asking

Prayers Answered 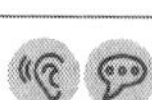

What pieces of armor were used to keep you UNDAUNTED?

DAY 63

Thanksgiving

God's Word

Praise & Worship

Humility & Confession

Put on the full armor of God so you can stand your ground!

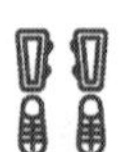

Reflection

The Asking

Prayers Answered

What pieces of armor were used to keep you UNDAUNTED?

DAY 64

Thanksgiving

Praise & Worship

Humility & Confession

God's Word

Put on the full armor of God so you can stand your ground!

Reflection

The Asking

Prayers Answered

What pieces of armor were used to keep you UNDAUNTED?

Thanksgiving

God's Word 

Praise & Worship 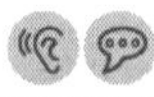

Humility & Confession 

Put on the full armor of God so you can stand your ground!

Reflection

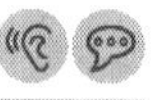

The Asking

Prayers Answered

What pieces of armor were used to keep you UNDAUNTED?

DAY 66

Thanksgiving

God's Word

Praise & Worship

Humility & Confession

Put on the full armor of God so you can stand your ground!

Reflection

The Asking

Prayers Answered

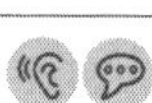

What pieces of armor were used to keep you UNDAUNTED?

DAY 67

Thanksgiving

Praise & Worship

Humility & Confession

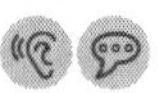

God's Word

Put on the full armor of God so you can stand your ground!

Reflection

The Asking

Prayers Answered

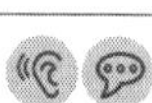

What pieces of armor were used to keep you UNDAUNTED?

Thanksgiving

Praise & Worship

Humility & Confession

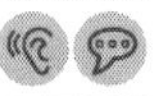

God's Word

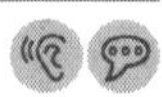

Put on the full armor of God so you can stand your ground!

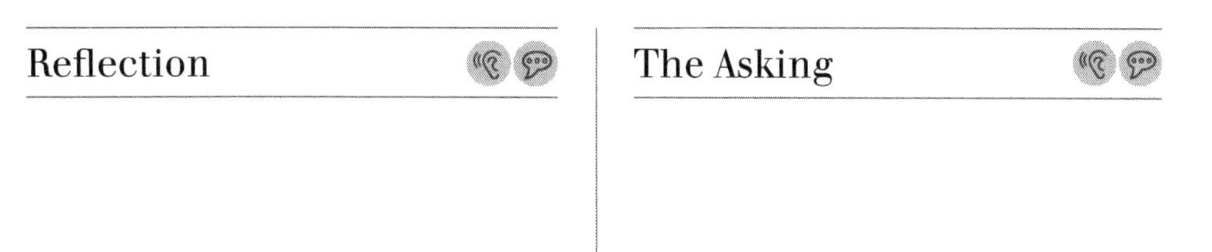

Reflection

The Asking

Prayers Answered

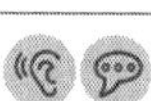

What pieces of armor were used to keep you UNDAUNTED?

Thanksgiving

Praise & Worship

Humility & Confession

God's Word

Put on the full armor of God so you can stand your ground!

Reflection

The Asking

Prayers Answered

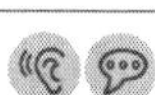

DAY 70

Thanksgiving

God's Word

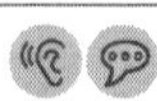

Praise & Worship

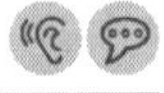

Humility & Confession

Put on the full armor of God so you can stand your ground!

Reflection

The Asking

Prayers Answered

What pieces of armor were used to keep you UNDAUNTED?

Thanksgiving

Praise & Worship

Humility & Confession

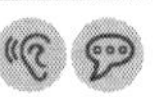

God's Word

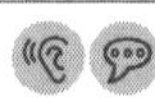

Put on the full armor of God so you can stand your ground!

Reflection

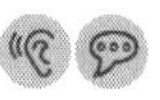

The Asking

Prayers Answered

What pieces of armor were used to keep you UNDAUNTED?

DAY 72

Thanksgiving

God's Word

Praise & Worship

Humility & Confession

Put on the full armor of God so you can stand your ground!

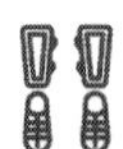

Reflection

The Asking

Prayers Answered

What pieces of armor were used to keep you UNDAUNTED?

DAY 73

Thanksgiving

Praise & Worship

Humility & Confession

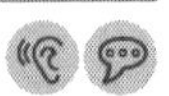

God's Word

Put on the full armor of God so you can stand your ground!

Reflection 

The Asking 

Prayers Answered 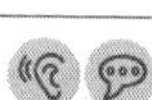

What pieces of armor were used to keep you UNDAUNTED?

DAY 74

Thanksgiving

God's Word

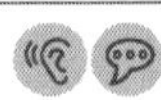

Praise & Worship

Humility & Confession

Put on the full armor of God so you can stand your ground!

Reflection

The Asking

Prayers Answered

What pieces of armor were used to keep you UNDAUNTED?

DAY 75

Thanksgiving

God's Word

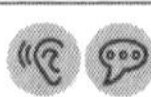

Praise & Worship

Humility & Confession

Put on the full armor of God so you can stand your ground!

Reflection

The Asking

Prayers Answered

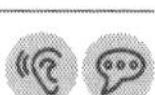

What pieces of armor were used to keep you UNDAUNTED?

DAY 76

Thanksgiving

Praise & Worship

Humility & Confession

God’s Word

Put on the full armor of God so you can stand your ground!

Reflection

The Asking

Prayers Answered

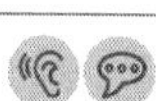

What pieces of armor were used to keep you UNDAUNTED?

Thanksgiving

Praise & Worship

Humility & Confession

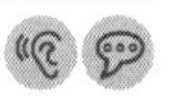

God's Word

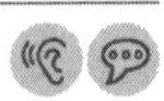

Put on the full armor of God so you can stand your ground!

Reflection

The Asking

Prayers Answered

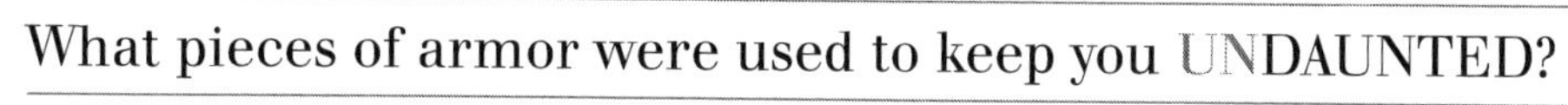

What pieces of armor were used to keep you UNDAUNTED?

DAY 78

Thanksgiving

Praise & Worship

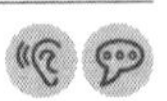

Humility & Confession

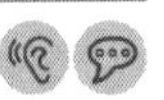

God's Word

Put on the full armor of God so you can stand your ground!

Reflection

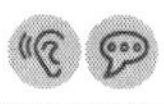

The Asking

Prayers Answered

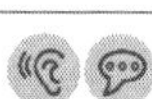

What pieces of armor were used to keep you UNDAUNTED?

DAY 79

Thanksgiving

Praise & Worship

Humility & Confession

God's Word

Put on the full armor of God so you can stand your ground!

Reflection

The Asking

Prayers Answered

What pieces of armor were used to keep you UNDAUNTED?

DAY 80

Thanksgiving

God's Word

Praise & Worship 

Humility & Confession 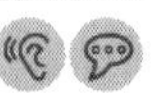

Put on the full armor of God so you can stand your ground!

Reflection

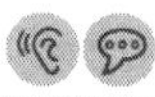

The Asking

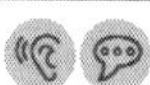

Prayers Answered

What pieces of armor were used to keep you UNDAUNTED?

DAY 81

Thanksgiving

God's Word

Praise & Worship

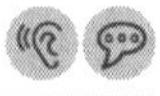

Humility & Confession

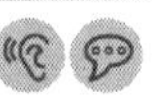

Put on the full armor of God so you can stand your ground!

Reflection

The Asking

Prayers Answered

What pieces of armor were used to keep you UNDAUNTED?

DAY 82

Thanksgiving

Praise & Worship

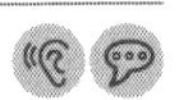

Humility & Confession

God's Word

Put on the full armor of God so you can stand your ground!

Reflection

The Asking

Prayers Answered

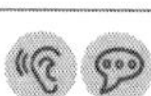

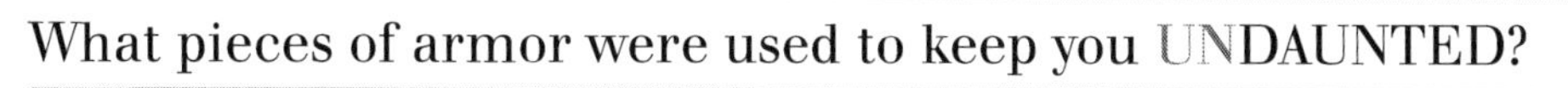

What pieces of armor were used to keep you UNDAUNTED?

DAY 83

Thanksgiving

God's Word

Praise & Worship

Humility & Confession

Put on the full armor of God so you can stand your ground!

Reflection

The Asking

Prayers Answered

What pieces of armor were used to keep you UNDAUNTED?

DAY 84

Thanksgiving

Praise & Worship

Humility & Confession

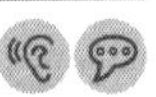

God’s Word

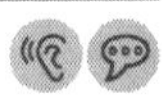

Put on the full armor of God so you can stand your ground!

Reflection

The Asking

Prayers Answered

DAY 85

Thanksgiving

God's Word

Praise & Worship

Humility & Confession

Put on the full armor of God so you can stand your ground!

Reflection

The Asking

Prayers Answered

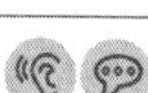

What pieces of armor were used to keep you UNDAUNTED?

DAY 86

Thanksgiving

Praise & Worship

Humility & Confession

God's Word

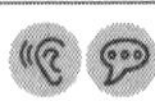

Put on the full armor of God so you can stand your ground!

Reflection

The Asking

Prayers Answered 

What pieces of armor were used to keep you UNDAUNTED?

Thanksgiving

Praise & Worship

Humility & Confession

God's Word

Put on the full armor of God so you can stand your ground!

Reflection

The Asking

Prayers Answered

What pieces of armor were used to keep you UNDAUNTED?

Thanksgiving

Praise & Worship

Humility & Confession

God's Word

Put on the full armor of God so you can stand your ground!

Reflection

The Asking

Prayers Answered

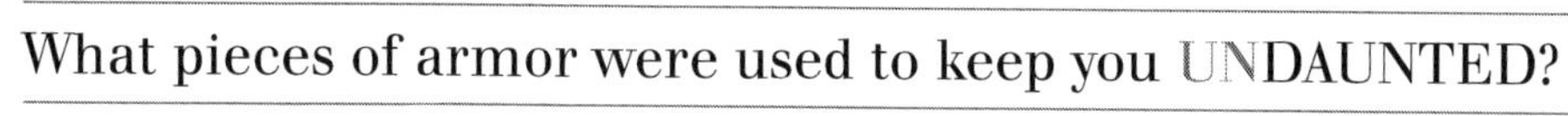

What pieces of armor were used to keep you UNDAUNTED?

Thanksgiving

Praise & Worship

Humility & Confession

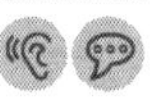

God’s Word

Put on the full armor of God so you can stand your ground!

Reflection

The Asking

Prayers Answered

What pieces of armor were used to keep you UNDAUNTED?

DAY 90

Thanksgiving 

Praise & Worship 

Humility & Confession 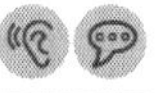

God's Word 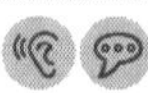

Put on the full armor of God so you can stand your ground!

Reflection

The Asking

Prayers Answered

What pieces of armor were used to keep you UNDAUNTED?

TESTIMONY

Congratulations. It's my hope that if you're reading this you've been communing with God through prayer in a deeper way. If you're reading here before the rest of the book, (I've done that before) it's okay because you can come back around after you've completed your journal pages. At any point in your reading, I would love to hear your testimony of how God is speaking to you and what He's revealed since the day you began. Here are some questions for you to give thought to.

Did your listening increase?

Which piece(s) of the armor of God did you use the most?

How has using this journal left you feeling UNDAUNTED?

IRON SHARPENS IRON

A friendly discussion is as stimulating
as the sparks that fly when iron strikes iron.

—PROVERBS 27:17 TLB

Let's connect through the UNDAUNTED online community. There we can share stories and encourage one another in our prayer journaling. Visit me for links to my social media groups at victoriachapin.com/.

ABOUT THE AUTHOR

Victoria Chapin is on a mission to embrace the truth found in John 10:10; Jesus came that we may have life and have it more abundantly. Her passion to do life to the full, despite life's trials, has inspired others to find hope and healing in Jesus. Victoria is a chaplain, speaker, and award-winning author, who is actively involved in ministry leadership focusing on grief, creative arts, and women's ministries. She currently serves on the board of directors for Starlight Ministries and as co-director for The Well Ministry for Creatives. Victoria is blessed to be mom to twelve and a grammy to thirteen grandchildren. She and her husband Jim make their home in southwest Michigan.

Made in the USA
Columbia, SC
07 November 2021